A DYING MAN'S REGRETS

ADOLPHE MONOD

an extract from
Adolphe Monod's Farewell to his Friends and to his Church

GREAT CHRISTIAN BOOKS
LINDENHURST, NEW YORK

A GREAT CHRISTIAN BOOK

A Dying Man's Regrets

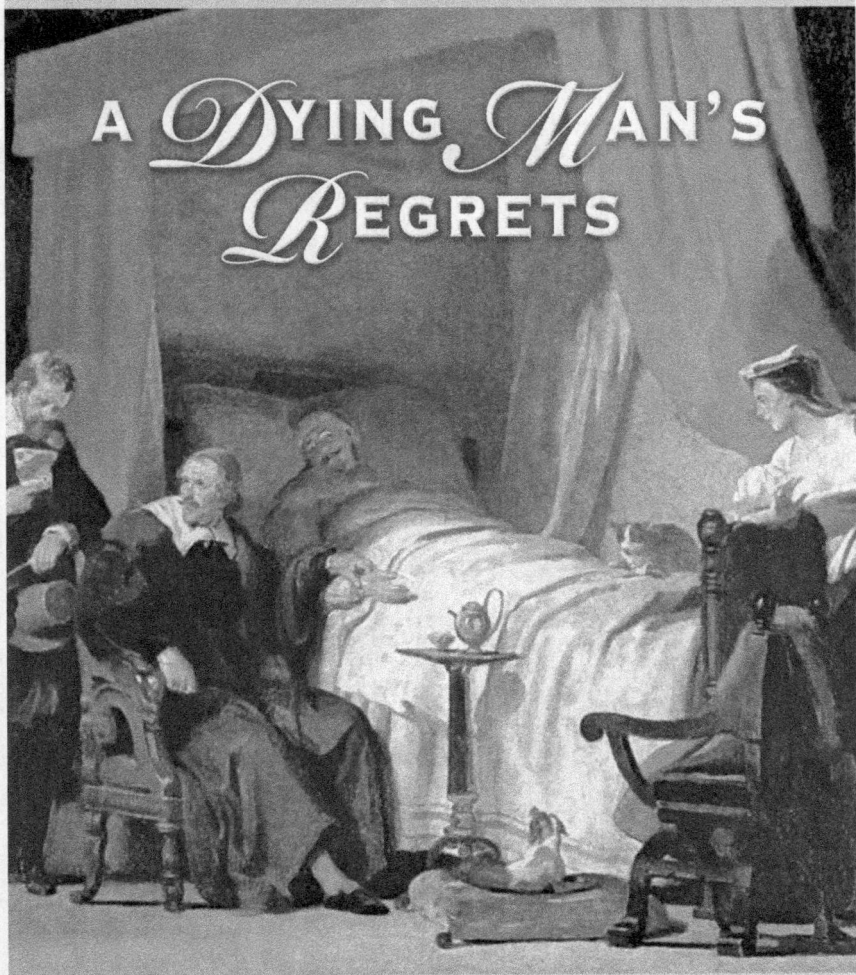

Adolphe Monod

A GREAT CHRISTIAN BOOKS publication
Great Christian Books is an imprint of Rotolo Media
160 37th Street Lindenhurst, New York 11757
(631) 956-0998
www.GreatChristianBooks.com
email: mail@greatchristianbooks.com
A Dying Man's Regrets   ISBN 978-1-61010-000-7

Monod, Adolphe, 1802–1856
    A Dying Man's Regrets / by Adolphe Monod
    p.   cm.
A "A Great Christian Book" book
GREAT CHRISTIAN BOOKS an imprint of Rotolo Media
ISBN 978-1-61010-000-7
Recommended Dewey Decimal Classification: 234
Suggested Subject Headings:
1. Religion—Christian literature—Adolphe Monod
2. Christianity—The Bible—Christian Living
I. Title

The book and cover design for this title are by Michael Rotolo
(www.michaelrotolo.com). It is typeset in the Minion and Myriad
typefaces by Adobe Inc. and is quality manufactured in the United
States on premium, archival quality acid-free paper stock. To discuss
the publication of your Christian manuscript or out-of-print book,
please contact Great Christian Books. www.greatchristianbooks.com

MANUFACTURED IN THE GREAT UNITED STATES OF AMERICA

CONTENTS

PREFACE

When in September, 1855, Adolphe Monod was overtaken by a fatal illness it seemed that the earthly ministry of the foremost preacher in France had come to an end. His voice would no more rouse the thronged congregations in the Oratoire, Paris, as it had done for nine years past, and soon his life would no more be the "lighthouse," as a contemporary described him, "to whom everyone looked as the sailor in the storm." Thus suddenly reduced to the pain of a sick-bed at the age of fifty-three, Monod had but one concern: "O my God," he prayed, "is my work finished? Thou knowest... I should so much have wished to leave behind me some lasting monument for thy glory." His prayer was answered, yet not in the way he might have imagined. God did not restore him to his former work but brought him to exercise a new ministry—the ministry of suffering and patience which occasioned the contents of his book Adolphe Monod's Farewell to his Friends and to his Church. As long as evangelical literature is read, Monod's Farewell will be remembered as the most enduring monument he left to the glory of God.

The sudden termination of his fruitful ministry was a sore loss to France, yet with his opportunities for spiritual usefulness suddenly reduced to the dimensions of a single bedroom, Monod devoted the months that remained to the ministry that abides in the pages of his book. Commencing on October 14th, 1855, he began to partake the Lord's Supper with a varying company of friends who gathered in his room every Sunday afternoon. Too weak to speak for long and too ill to prepare anything more than a short meditation, Monod used these occasions to commend the Savior who now sustained him amidst incessant suffering. Knowing the time was short, his light shone brighter—no longer as an eloquent preacher but as a suffering saint nearing his end—and if the radiance of things eternal falls on the reader as he goes through the following chapters it is because the author was daily entering into deeper communion with Him who has brought "immortality and life to light."

These pages were neither written nor corrected by Monod; but they are the words of his short discourses taken down carefully as he spoke and purposely left in their original spontaneous form. By their literary form as well as by their peculiar unction and power, we are thus reminded that Monod spoke as a dying man to dying men.

The delivery of these exhortations continued for nearly six months, though they were often the means of aggravating his physical sufferings. On March 23rd he gave his last address on The Resurrection of Christ—though in such weakness that he seemed ready to faint in pronouncing the closing words. The following Sunday, March 30th, "scarcely knowing whether he should be able to make himself heard, he collected the little strength he had to glorify the everlasting and infinite love of God," and terminated with a prayer of thanksgiving his ministry upon earth. Before the sun had set on the following Lord's Day, April 6th, 1856, Monod had entered "the land of pure delight where saints immortal reign."

"More than anyone else," wrote Professor de Felice in his History of the French Protestants, "Adolphe Monod recalled to us the venerable image of the Christians of the primitive Church." That such a man, who spent the last twenty-five years of his lifer in whole-hearted devotion to Christ, found it necessary to speak so fully as he does in this book on A Dying Man's Regrets; is a sobering fact. Life in retrospect, under the shadow of a coming eternity, and weighed in the balances of Scripture, is an experience which all who read this book will one day share. Our present viewpoint will soon be changed—things that are temporal must give way to things eternal—and to realize these facts in advance is to heed the exhortation of the Apostle, "Abide in Him; that, when He shall appear, we may have confidence, and not be ashamed at His coming." (lst John 2:28)

—Iain Murray, August 1962, as extracted from the 1962 Banner of Truth edition of *Adolphe Monod's Farewell*

1

THE SECRET OF
A HOLY, ACTIVE &
PEACEFUL LIFE

My dearly beloved in the well-beloved of the Father, I thank God who again allows me to address you in His name, for your encouragement and for my own consolation; but I have great need that you have with me the patience of God, "with whom we are accepted according to that a man hath, and not according to that he hath not." My declining strength neither allows me to turn nor to raise myself, and it is only in this reclining position that I can speak to you. I hope to be able to do it so as to be heard by all.

A man is in a singular position who has been for a number of months, and may perhaps continue an indefinite time to come, constantly living under the impression that the bonds that held him to life are snapped—that God has struck him with an incurable and mortal disease, and he knows not how soon his Father's voice may call him home. He must, indeed, be insensible, and greatly wanting in reflection and Christian feeling, if he does not cast a retrospective look upon his past life; and at the same time, as thoughts of recovery ought and must rise in his mind—for, after all, he is in the hands of God, who can raise the dead, and who has raised many nearer death than he—he is disposed to ask himself, If I were restored to life, what use should I make of it? And while he recollects, that his whole life has proved the weakness and frailty of his resolutions, still he hopes that, by the goodness of God, such a visitation would not be lost for the second portion of his life and of his ministry. And then he says, I should like to do such or such a thing; and certainly there is nothing that I should not wish to do differently and better than I have done it. This is a cause of salutary humiliation for me; it may be a salutary instruction for you to reflect upon the regrets of a man who is dying, or who believes himself to be dying, and who seeks to represent to himself the different use he would make of life if it were restored to him.

It is more particularly towards such thoughts as these that I wish to draw your attention upon these occasions; and in order to choose immediately an example, there are points upon which, if I were to begin life anew, I would make considerable changes— I mean in my spiritual life. Of course, the private applications of the principle I have laid down belong to the Lord; but there are general applications of it that may be mentioned without inconvenience in a small meeting like this—for instance, prayer, the reading of the Bible, Christian liberty.

Now, here is a thing that strikes me. *I regret having regulated my life too much upon my own plans*—I mean upon my plans of faithfulness and Christian sanctification—and not more simply upon the plan that the Lord unfolds before each of us. I think I can easily make you understand my idea in a few words, and every child of God will be ready to apprehend it immediately. We are disposed to form for ourselves a certain ideal of Christian life, of Christian activity, and of a Christian ministry, and to attach to our ideal certain plans and methods, and we are satisfied with ourselves only if we can attain to the realization of them. It is, then, of importance to make the best plans, and to seek the best methods possible for their execution. All this is undoubtedly very good; but there is a great defect at the root of it: self—hidden self—which is so deeply rooted in the heart, and but too evidently appears in our best and purest works. What I should wish, would be to form the plan of my life, and of my daily conduct, not according to my own ideas, nor my own feelings, but according to the commandments of God, to His inward witness, to the guiding of His Spirit, and to the outward direction He gives to our life.

My ideas of the manner in which I would regulate my life will be easily understood by those who reflect upon the way in which Jesus regulated His. We do not find in Jesus those plans and methods that have so much occupied many good people, and have often perplexed them, and taken up a considerable part of their time which might have been better employed, But what do we find? We find a man (I consider Him here as the Son of man) who has no other wish than to accomplish the mission He has received from the Father, and who has no other plan than to enter into the plans of the Father; so that, with His eyes constantly fixed upon Him, He is only occupied in listening to His voice, that He may follow its directions, and to discern His will, in order to execute it. The works of Jesus Christ are prepared for Him one after another, and set by God before Him on His way,

11

following each other so naturally, and arising so easily one out of another, that they never occasioned any confusion, even in the busiest days of His ministry. On a day, for instance, like that described in the ninth chapter of Saint Matthew, in which He calls one of His apostles, heals several sick, restores to life a dead child, and, as He was passing by, heals a woman who had been diseased several years, without mentioning the other good deeds which He spread all along upon His way, there is not an instant of hesitation or embarrassment, either for the arrangement of these works or for the time given to each, because Jesus Christ followed the plan of God, and God led Him by a straight path. Whenever there is on man's part this perfect accordance with the will of God, God on His part leads us in perfect light. And thus is realized an admirable and profound expression of the Holy Spirit: "We are created in Jesus Christ unto good works, which God hath prepared that we should walk in them." Here good works are presented, not as a path that we have to make out for ourselves, but as a path that God has traced, and in which we have only to walk. It is God's way, not our own; we have only to follow this path, and we shall perform every moment the will of God. If I have made you understand as well as I could, with so little development, what I wish I had done, and what I wish to do if restored to life, you will easily see the advantage that this conformity of our will with the will of God has over our personal plans, even the best of them. I must add, that I have no wish to discourage personal plans, which we should always endeavour to make as complete as possible. I think that our weakness requires this prop, provided our personal plans are always subordinate to the general rule of following only the will of God.

Now, to mention two or three principal ideas, the method of which Jesus Christ gives us an example, is, in the first place, a condition of holiness. What constitutes sin, taken in its primitive sense? It is the seeking of self, self-confidence, self-will, self-righteousness, self-glory—and of all that relates to us personally. So the wish to do what is right, and even to do the Lord's will, if it is only founded upon our own will and projects, inevitably participates in some measure of the root of sin; while, on the contrary, the very essence of holiness being the conformity of our will with the Divine will, it is when we have no other plan than that of God, and no other will than the will of God, that we shall have attained true holiness—holiness that will not appear outwardly only, but that will have an inward influence—a holiness like that of Jesus Christ. The holiness of Jesus Christ follows and results from the principle I have just mentioned; that is to say, a constant surrender to the will of God alone, manifested inwardly by the testimony of His Spirit, and outwardly by the declarations of His Word and by the indications of His providence. Jesus Christ is holy, because He wills only what God wills—because He seeks not His own glory, but that of the Father. This is the power of His holiness.

This conformity to the will of God is, then, a condition of holiness, and it is at the same time a condition of activity. Much time may be lost in seeking to please ourselves even in what is good. It is well to recollect how easily we may be mistaken, and how we may be absorbed in endless reflections and considerations. But how many men have acknowledged at the end of their career, that a considerable part of their life has been spent in forming plans, that might have been more usefully employed in accomplishing the work immediately at hand, and promoting thus the good of others! See what activity the plan followed by Jesus Christ, that I have just mentioned, allows Him. In the ninth chapter of Saint Matthew and elsewhere, we see good works thrown in His way, not one upon another, but one after another; and there is no limit to an activity founded upon this perfect harmony with the will of God, the action of man becoming a Divine action, and his life, as it were, becoming a Divine life, implanted in our human nature, in which something of the power of God is wrought. We have no idea of what we could do if self were completely swallowed up in this perfect harmony with God, if we sought no other will than His; if every word of our mouth, every throb of our heart, every thought of our mind, every movement of our spirit or body, were drawn towards Him, saying, "Speak, Lord, for thy servant heareth." Some men have shewn what man can do—Luther, Calvin, Saint Paul, Moses; these men shewed what a man can do, when he seeks only the will of God. Jesus Christ did much more, because in Him alone the conformity with the Divine will was perfect. It is, then, a condition of activity—of almost unlimited activity; yet there is a limit, since God does not require of His creatures more than they are capable of doing.

Finally, and I here conclude, it is a condition of peace. There is no peace for a man who makes self his mainspring of action. There is always fear that he may be mistaken; he is troubled, and often commits errors, because human will and human interests are subject to much error; he can find no rest, he is agitated, tormented, and excites the profound compassion of him who, seeing the sincere desire lie has to glorify God, sees at the same time how many obstacles his want of simplicity accumulates around his way; while, on the contrary, when we look to God alone, we can cast our burden upon Him, and He will sustain us.

And again, if my plans are of my own imagining, they may not be practicable. I wish to embrace a profession, but a certain expenditure, that I cannot meet, would be requisite.

I wish to be a painter, but my sight is not good; or an orator, but I have no voice; or a surgeon, but my hand trembles. All my hopes are disappointed, arid I shall never be consoled. But there could be no such disappointment if my projects were chosen in accordance with God's appointed plan. If they were, the impossibility of doing what I had at first intended, would shew me that what I wished was not what God called me to; and the obstacles that rise in my way are like so many lights, by which God reveals to me my true vocation. If we act in this spirit (I say it with deep reverence), our vocation is God's affair rather than our own—it is His work, and not ours; and the activity, the individual exertion that God always requires of us, consists only in following where He leads, in a spirit of faithful and childlike obedience. In that we shall find perfect peace. God cannot mislead us. We are often tormented with the thought, that we do not do enough, or that we do amiss, or that we do not do the work which God appointed for us.

During the first weeks that followed the declaration of the doctors (that my disease was beyond their skill), I recollect how much I was troubled by the idea that my work was not done. By the grace of God I am now delivered from these thoughts, because I understand that is not my work, but God's; and I acknowledge that, by the sufferings and the afflictions He has sent me, and by the hope of eternal life that will follow, the Lord teaches me to exercise a new ministry, probably a more important one than what I had purposed, and at all events more sure, because it comes more directly from the hand of God, who mercifully constrains me to walk in this path for His service and glory. It is in such cases that we can say, like Jesus Christ before He suffered death, "I have finished the work thou gavest me to do." And why could He say that? Because He sought only to do the work of God, and God withdrew

Him, as a ripe fruit is gathered, when His mission was accomplished. Well, and snail not we, too, seek to do the work that the Father has given us to do, committing ourselves to His care. And if we are faithful, we also shall only be withdrawn when our work is accomplished. To God alone it belongs to decide when the work He will do by us is accomplished. It may be imperfect, incomplete in the judgment of men; but if we are upright before Him, the Lord will not allow us to pass away without leaving any trace behind us upon the earth; He will not withdraw us before our work is accomplished in His sight; and we shall be enabled to say, in a spirit of humility, with the Lord, "I have finished the work that thou gavest me to do." Vinet said so, without being aware of it, when he gave his last theological lecture upon these words, "I have finished the work that thou gavest me to do." And what was accomplished in Vinet, was also in Rochat, and in all the true servants of God. There is much peace in seeking our plans only in God, and in following Him, denying ourselves; and it is only thus peace is to be found.

Let us, then, endeavour to seek our plans in God alone; that those who are summoned away may humble themselves, and those who have still to live may grow in grace. Let us in this spirit endeavour to follow Jesus Christ in His Gethsemane, having our eyes constantly fixed upon the Father's will. It will be for us as it was for Jesus Christ, a condition of holiness, a condition of activity, and a condition of perfect peace. It is this peace that I ask of God for you, and I should be happy if I could think that these few reflections have excited in those who have still before them life and strength the wish to use them faithfully, and simply to glorify God according to their Saviour's example, so that they may be able to say, when their turn comes, "I have finished the work that thou gavest me to do," and may spend in perfect peace the time that intervenes till they are called from this world to the Father, by the grace of the Lord, and by the power and unction of the Holy Spirit.

2

THE STUDY OF THE
WORD OF GOD

My dear friends, last Sunday I began to shew you, under the title of the regrets of a dying man, the views he then takes of many things that he wishes he had done otherwise than he has, and of the way in which he would do them if he were recalled to life from his half-opened tomb. Among the ideas suggested by this subject, one of the most important is the way in which ne has studied the Word of God. Ah! he certainly then says, How differently I ought to have acted with regard to the Word of God! how much more I ought to have studied it! how much better I ought now to be acquainted with it, to be both better able at the same time to put in practice its precepts, and to communicate it to others. Let us pause a few moments upon this salutary subject, to hum Die those for whom the end of time approaches, and to enlighten those to whom time is yet given, but who know not for how long.

What are the Holy Scriptures? Men can never precisely explain the manner in which they were composed, nor, in particular, how the Spirit of God and the spirit of man are combined in them so as to make them at the same time Divine and human—a Divine word reaching to heaven, and at the same time human, and quite near to us. This is not less difficult to explain than the manner in which the Divine and human nature were united in Jesus Christ. This parallel is not mine, for Scripture calls itself the written Word, and it calls Jesus Christ the "Word made flesh." But however the Holy Scriptures may have been composed, "they literally are heaven speaking upon earth; "they are the maxims of the kingdom of heaven communicated to men in human language, as if the invisible world were come down amongst them, and placed before their eyes. There is no other book, even amongst the best, which like this makes known to us the mysteries of the kingdom of heaven. All are more or less tainted with human errors: this alone is exempt from them. It is the took of God, full of the truth of God; in it we hear God speak by the Holy Spirit. We see God, man—the present, the future—time and eternity, described exactly as they are.

For any one who has thus understood what Scripture is, it will not be difficult to confess the use he ought to make of it. We ought to interrogate the Scriptures as we would an angel from heaven, sent by God at this very moment on purpose to instruct us; or, what is still better, as we would question the Lord Jesus Christ if we could speak to Him and hear Him. And, in fact, we do speak to Him and hear Him when we read the Holy Scriptures, for they reveal Him, and through Him they reveal all things by His Spirit.

Oh! how can we sufficiently love and venerate this book? It is true it is not the book that saves us, but it is the book that reveals the way of salvation, without which we could never have known it; and by which, the better we know it, the better we shall know Jesus the Saviour of our souls. No Christian will contest the truth of this principle, and yet how few there are who really study the Scriptures! The greater number read them superficially, and are satisfied with knowing some great leading truths, without penetrating more deeply into them, and as far as possible really understanding them in all things, as it is written: "The secret things belong unto the Lord our God; but those things which are revealed belong unto us and to our children for ever." And why this strange contradiction with our own convictions? It arises from the difficulties that the study of the Bible presents. We must acknowledge that on beginning it there are many difficulties and much obscurity. Some labour is necessary to dissipate them; and as the mind of man is naturally slow and idle, and he easily loses courage, and is satisfied with reading over and over again without penetrating further than the surface, so he learns nothing new, and the constant perusal of the same things causes weariness, as if the Word of God were not interesting—as if we could not always find some new instruction in it—as if it were not inexhaustible as God himself! Let us, however, beware of thinking these difficulties insurmountable. No, my friends, but we must give ourselves trouble; for here, as in every part of the Christian life, God will have us to be labourers with himself. And the knowledge of the Bible, a relish for the Bible, are the fruit and recompense of this humble^ sincere, and persevering labour.

Ah! then, let every one return to his Bible with renewed courage. Take book after book, seeking not only to gather from your study a general idea of outward piety, but a deep and growing knowledge of the kingdom of heaven. Study a book till you understand it as well as you can, and then take a second, and a third, and so on, and you will find on a second or third reading many difficulties that seemed insurmountable disappear, and even though some should remain, you will not profit the less by this labour, patiently undertaken before God. In this study, you must not except the most difficult books, such as the prophets— the minor prophets, that many Christians pass by as unintelligible; but if you take the trouble to study them, you will find much in them that is very interesting.

Besides, there are, through the goodness of God, many books that may be useful—commentaries upon certain portions of Scripture—that are as a key to other parts, and by the help of them we may penetrate more and more into the knowledge of the Word of God. Then we may give more attention to those parts of the book more especially addressed to Christians, but, I repeat it, without neglecting any part. The fruit and the recompense of those who are thus faithful and persevering in understanding the Word of God, will be to love it—to penetrate more and more deeply into it—and to find the time always too short for becoming well acquainted with it.

I know a man who spent seven hours every day in the study of the Bible, and he always found increasing charms in it. If any one in faith, making use of the resources that God gives him, and looking to God for guidance, should carry out these rules, which it is impossible for me to do more than indicate, he will find in the Word of God treasures of which he has no idea. It will be for him as firm a support as it was for Jesus when He was tempted in the desert. It will become for him what it was for all the saints of the New Testament, and for those of the Old Testament, as regards those portions of Scripture which existed before them—what it was for David— what it was for Daniel—what it was for Saint Paul— what it always has been for all the saints of God. May God grant us all this grace; and may He to whom it is not more difficult to bless in a short than in a longer time, nor with little strength than with much strength, so make the words that I address to you penetrate into your hearts, that they may cause a transformation in your plan of studying the Bible, for which you will bless God through all eternity! Amen.

3

THE USE OF TIME

My strength is exhausted, my dear friends, and it was a question with me whether I should not keep silence today: I shall, however, say to you what I intended, doing it as briefly as I can.

One of the things that trouble, or that would trouble, the Christian who thinks himself near his end, if he were not at the foot of the cross, is the manner in which he has employed his time: it is consequently one of the subjects of the exhortations that he addresses to his brethren who have life before them. It is written, "Redeem the opportunity; "this version is more correct than the received one, "Redeeming the time." To redeem does not here signify to buy a second time, but to seize eagerly the opportunities that God offers us, "because the days are evil," so that an opportunity missed can never return. The good use of time, taken in a general sense, is an idea so vast that it overawes; it will be more suitable here to take it in this more limited sense, and say, Lay hold eagerly of opportunities as God causes them to arise in your path. How much time, how many opportunities are lost by idleness or unbelief—by negligence or selfishness—by self-will or hesitation—by love of sin, or by a thousand other causes. It is not necessary to pause long here, for there is no Christian whose heart and conscience do not accuse him upon this point. The time that God gives us is precious and sufficient. God, who is just, measures the time to the work, and the work to the time; and never gives us a good action to perform for which the time is lacking, nor a moment of our existence in which we have not something good to do. But how can we attain to thus filling up all our time, and doing at least some part of the immense good that a man might do if he put in practice the precept, "Whatsoever thy hand findeth to do, do it with all thy might," and if he were constantly occupied in serving the Lord? I wish to submit to you a few thoughts on the subject, leaving it to your conscience to develop them.

1. We must be deeply impressed with the conviction that we are not our own—that our time is not our own, but, like all the rest we have, belongs to God, and it is consequently in God that we ought always to seek what we have to do in order to fill up the time He gives us, and take advantage of the opportunities that He offers us. I assure you that sickness gives precious lessons upon this point: I mean upon the fact that we do not belong to ourselves, but to God. Our heart is naturally disposed (and this is the very root of sin) to constitute itself the centre and aim of life. But in sickness and suffering how can we find consolation if we seek in seethe aim of life? The aim of life is then completely lost. Sickness teaches us that we must seek it elsewhere; that we do not live in order to be happy upon the earth, but we live to glorify God, which we can do in sickness as well as in health, and

often still better. Let us then learn from sickness, from all the sufferings of life, and from the whole Word of God, that our time belongs to God, and that all we have to do is to employ it to His glory.

2. Let us always be ready diligently to seize the opportunities that God offers us; they will not be wanting; and we shall find before us a life interwoven with good works prepared and ready, in which we shall only have to walk, and which will be so well and easily linked together, that our life will wholly be made up of good works and obedience, and consequently, as has just been said, of peace and joy in the Holy Spirit. For this we must have our eyes constantly opened and turned towards God, saying, Lord, here I am, what wilt thou have me to do? And when we have done one thing, Lord, what wilt thou have me to do now? and so on, without a single interval not filled up with the obedience due to God; and God will in this way furnish us with the means of doing an incalculable amount of good. No one can estimate the good that might enter into the life of a single man regulated by such a disposition,—witness the man Jesus Christ. Even in the things of this world, the men that have done the most are those that have lived on this principle of seizing opportunities. If you study carefully the lives of the men who have accomplished the most considerable and numerous works, such as Calvin, Luther, Bossuet, you will see that they undertook things according as they presented themselves and came in their way, and that they were men called by circumstances gradually to do what they accomplished; as Bossuet, for instance, was led by the requirements of the Dauphin's education to compose his best works; as, likewise, Calvin and Luther wrote their best works when called to do so by particular circumstances: while, on

the contrary, ordinary men who do little are those who do not know how to profit by passing opportunities. They might perhaps have done as much as others who have accomplished a great deal, but they had not the art of laying hold of the opportunity; and the true art of seizing the opportunity is the Christian art of having the eyes always turned towards the Lord, and thus being ready to undertake each work as Pie provides it, and when one work is done, to go on to another. It is prodigious what can be accomplished in the life of a man in simply following the path that the Lord opens before each of us.

3. We must regulate our actions with order and method, and not abandon to chance the use of the time that God gives us. I said some days ago that we should not make plans for ourselves; but there is no contradiction in saying that we ought to act with method, provided our method is undertaken in the Lord. To do what God gives us to do, there must be method and order. It is desirable to have regular hours for rising in the morning and for our work; to be as exact as possible in the hours at which we take our meals, and in all our various occupations. Life then becomes much more simple and easy; it is like a well-adjusted framework, in which the Lord has only to act. The men who have done the most are those who know best how to regulate calmly and steadily their course of life, especially if they know how to add to their firmness an activity of mind and a warmth of heart that do not always accompany a spirit of order and method, but which, when combined, enable a man to do the most astonishing things. It is said that Kant, the philosopher, sometimes amused himself in calling his servant, and taking him to witness that for forty years he had risen every morning

regularly at four o'clock. Think what a man may do who rises every morning at that hour, and then think of the beneficial results of method, independently of the early hour of rising. From the fact of having a regular hour for rising, how much more time shall I not have to consecrate to the Lord, for the simple reason of my having fixed the hour in a spirit of prayer before God, taking into account the dictates of Christian prudence and wisdom; while, on the contrary, if I rise at any hour, the time will be regulated only by the impulse of the moment, that is to say, by various circumstances over which I might have triumphed—by my idleness, my desire of a little more sleep, "a little folding of the hands to sleep; so shall thy poverty come as one that travelleth," and not only poverty of money, but of mind, of labour, and of the service of God. Thus, method, and a life peacefully regulated before the Lord, is a thing of the highest importance to enable us to do much for the service of God.

And finally, not unnecessarily to multiply reflections, let us keep our bodies and minds in such a disposition as will bring no hindrance to that good use of time, and of the gifts we have received, to be employed in a way agreeable to God. Sadness, unevenness of temper, the seduction of self-will, the desire of human glory, are so many obstacles that surround and harass us unceasingly, and over which we must triumph. Then we must not neglect the body. Delicate health or weakness of body are often a great obstacle in the accomplishment of our work for God. We must accept these infirmities when God sends them, but it is our duty to take all the necessary precautions to strengthen our bodies for His service and glory: this idea elevates and sanctifies everything. Many men might have accomplished much more than they did for the glory of God, if they had not given themselves up to an activity in which there was more of piety than reflection, and which wore them out while they were young; and those who die young should examine if they have not to reproach themselves with the neglect of certain simple and easy precautions, in which it is difficult always to persevere, but that would have allowed them to labour longer for the service of God. But above all let us be careful to strengthen the mind and soul, and to avoid all that may fetter the work that God will accomplish in us and by us.

My friends, none of us know how long God may still leave us here, but we know the time He has already given us, and the reproaches that we deserve for the use we have made of it. Let us lay hold upon the portion still remaining before us, whether strong or weak, sick or in health, living or dying. We have a Saviour, every moment of whose time was engaged in obedience to God: let us follow His footsteps to glory by the cross, and at the end we shall hear that loving voice saying, "Well done, good and faithful servant; thou hast been faithful over a few things, I will make thee ruler over many things."

4

PRAYER

My dear friends in Christ, amongst the subjects towards which the regrets of the Christian who thinks himself near his end turn, there is certainly not one in which he would make a greater change, if he were to return to life, than in his habits of prayer. What is prayer, in practice and in reality, for the greater number of Christians—I mean of those who believe and who pray? Some moments given to retirement for prayer in the morning, some moments in the evening, the time being longer or shorter according to circumstances, and sometimes very short; then the heart lifted up to God under extraordinary circumstances, in which special need of drawing near to Him is felt;—it is to such narrow limits as these that the habits of many Christians, or" men who call themselves by this name, are restricted. It is for this reason that the fruits of prayer so often promised in Scripture are so little known to the greater number! Where are to be found those powerful fruits of sanctification that enable the soul to triumph over all temptations, like Jesus in the desert, making us more than conquerors in Him who loved us? Where are those fruits of consolation that diffuse into the soul a sweet and profound joy, capable of rising above the afflictions of the earth, so that even in the greatest anguish and bitterness, whether of the spirit, soul, or body, we are still able to rejoice in that perfect joy that Jesus, dying, desired for His disciples who were to live a dying life? Where are those fruits of deliverance in which the soul obtains from God what it asks, whether it say with Jesus, "I know that thou nearest me always," or, not being able to rise so high, it can say with David, "I have called upon thee, for thou wilt hear me"? Let us be sincere, and acknowledge that between the promises made in Scripture to prayer, and the fruits that we reap, the distance is so great that our feeble faith has more than once been troubled, and perhaps even shaken, and we have been tempted to say, And is that all? No, it is not all that was promised—but we have not done all that was commanded. Ah! my friends, prayer such as I have shewn you is very different from prayer such as the Scriptures shew it, and to which all the promises are made.

What is not prayer in the scriptural sense? I said some days ago that the Holy Scriptures, the Word of God, is Heaven speaking: continuing the figure, I now say that prayer, as described in Scripture, is Heaven abiding in us by the Holy Spirit. Without the Word, prayer is nothing, having no food, Without prayer, the Word is insufficient, because it does not penetrate into the heart. But when the heavenly truths with which the Scriptures abound are received, and, assimilated with the very substance of our souls by prayer, penetrate into our inner man, we then know that prayer brings within us Heaven, and all its blessings—the Holy Spirit, and all His graces—God, and all His promises. Prayer is the key that God has put into our hands, to open a communication for us with the invisible world: by it, we have everything; without it, nothing. I say, the key that God has put into our hands; for He has another key that He keeps in His own, and that He sometimes deigns to use for opening to us the invisible world, when we have neglected to open it for ourselves, that we might enter into communion with Him, and participate in His Divine proceedings, as it is written, "We are labourers together with God." Thus God, casting down Saul upon the way to Damascus, and raising him up a new man, opened heaven to him—when Saul, far from seeking Him, sought the disciples of Christ to torture them, and finally to put them to death. But these are extraordinary manifestations of the grace of God, upon which we ought not to reckon, and on which the more we reckon the less will they be granted. There can be no doubt that in all these extraordinary effects of the grace of God, we shall find, if we examine closely, sincerity in the soul that seeks. Saul of Tarsus, who went about persecuting the name of Jesus in His followers, was sincere in seeking God and His truth; and perhaps from the time that Saint Stephen prayed, for those that were putting him to death, a new life had begun to dawn in the soul of Saul. However that may be, we know that God's ordinary way of proceeding is to grant His favours in answer to prayer, and to wait for prayer before He grants them. Isaiah says, "And therefore will the Lord wait that he may be gracious unto you." And what does He wait for? He waits till you have cried unto Him. And in Jeremiah: "Then shall ye call upon me, and ye shall go and pray unto me, and I will hearken, and ye shall seek me, and find me, when ye shall search for me with all your heart." And so it is with us. It is by prayer that we can obtain everything; and it is to true prayer, such as the Scriptures describe, that all the promises are made.

Thus we see, my friends, that prayer is the distinctive mark of the Lord's mighty servants. With considerable differences, they all have this common feature—they are men who pray much and who pray fervently. Consider the prayers of Jacob:

he wrestled with the Lord a whole night, till he had prevailed over the Lord himself, who allowed him thus to triumph in order to exercise the faith of His servant. Consider the prayers of Moses and Samuel: of Moses, the lawgiver of Israel—of Samuel, the reformer in Israel; of whom Jeremiah says in the beginning of his fifteenth chapter, to shew that God had resolved not to grant a certain grace, "Though Moses and Samuel stood before me, yet my mind could not be toward this people." And now, let us try to substitute our own name for that of Moses or Samuel. Though such or such a one amongst us should have prayed, the petition would not be granted.... What a fall! What a humiliation! What a contradiction! Consider the prayers of David:—the Psalms—those prayers that were able to support, not only himself, but which are like the hundred and fifty pillars that have sustained generation after generation, and that will sustain all the generations of the people of God to the end of the world! Consider the prayers of King Jehoshaphat, who overthrew by prayer alone the combined armies of the Moabites, the Ammonites, and the inhabitants of Mount Seir; and of King Hezekiah, his great grandson and follower, who by prayer alone called down the exterminating vengeance of God upon an army of a hundred and eighty-five thousand men, who were only wailing for a good opportunity utterly to destroy Jerusalem. Consider the prayers of Nehemiah and Ezra, to raise arid reform their people, like Moses and Samuel, the one reviving the spiritual state and restoring the observance of the law, the other rebuilding the walls of Jerusalem and re-establishing its civil constitution. Consider the prayers of Jesus, the "author and finisher of our faith," who though He was Jesus, though He was the Son of God, nevertheless prayed,—spent whole nights in prayer, and did nothing but by prayer. By prayer

He appoints the apostolic body; by prayer He supports His apostles; by prayer He triumphs over the devil in the desert, in Gethsemane, and at Golgotha; by prayer he accomplishes the whole work of our redemption, having been rendered capable of suffering inconceivable pain, of which our sufferings, even the most excruciating, are scarcely able to give us the faintest image. And after Jesus, consider a new succession of men of prayer. Paul—what a giant in prayer! Prayer is the soul and spring of all his labour. Paul is Paul above all by means of prayer. Consider the prayers of Saint Augustine; the prayers of Calvin; of Luther, who, when he appeared before the Diet of Worms, passed three hours, taken from the best part of the day, in crying aloud to God, not knowing that his faithful friend Dietrich was indiscreetly listening at his door, to gather for the good of the Church those burning prayers.[1] Consider the prayers of Pascal, who, though suffering when

---

[1] Speaking of a residence at Cobourg, during the Diet of Augsburg, Dietrich thus writes to Melancthon:—" I cannot sufficiently admire his firmness, his joy, his faith, arid his hope, in these times of desolation. Every day he becomes, by constant application to the Word of God, more firm in his convictions. He never passes a day without reserving at least three hours for prayer, taken in the part of the day the most favourable to his work. One day I had the privilege of hearing him pray. Great God! what force, what faith in his words! He prays with all the respect of a man who is in the presence of God, but with all the confidence of a child speaking to his father. 'I know,' said he, 'that Thou art our good God and our Father, and therefore I am persuaded that Thou wilt exterminate those that persecute Thy children. If Thou do not, the danger is as great for Thee as for us. It is Thy cause; what we have done we could not have left undone. It is Thou, merciful Father, that must protect us." While I listened to him praying in a loud, clear voice in these words, my heart burned with joy within me, for I heard him speak to God with as much fervour as liberty: he rested so firmly upon the promises of the Psalms, that he seemed assured that nothing he asked could fail of being accomplished.

still young the most cruel and unremitting pains, is enabled to overcome them with a fortitude and a piety which we find deeply impressed in those beautiful and fervent prayers of his that have been handed down to us. Consider prayer in all the saints of every age; it is their faith, their life, the mainspring of all their actions,—their work.

Oh! my friends, I know not if you will be as deeply humbled as I am by these reflections. For my part, I cannot express to what a degree I am humbled when I think what my prayers have been compared with what they ought to have been—with what they might have been. We should certainly be, in our humble sphere of action, what these men were in the history of Scripture and of the Church, if we knew how to pray as they prayed, and if instead of saying, God granted them special privileges, we knew how to say,—

"Lord, teach me to pray." Ah! if I were to return to life, I would, with the help of God and in distrust of myself, give much more time to prayer than I have hitherto done, reckoning much more upon the effect of that than -on my own labour; which, however, it is our duty never to neglect, but which has no strength but in as far as it is animated by prayer. I would especially strive to obtain in my prayers that unction—that fervor of the Holy Spirit which is not learned in a day, but is the fruit of a long, and often a painful apprenticeship. O my friends! you who are full of life—you whose career does not seem to be near the end—though of that we know nothing, and I may live longer than you—lay hold of the opportunity and redeem it—cultivate new habits of prayer. Bring into prayer, with a spirit of fervor, a spirit of order and method that will increase its power, as it increases the power of all human things, and cooperates with the Divine agency itself; that method and arrangement of which Jesus Christ has given us an example in the model he left us—the Lord's prayer.

And, finally, pray God to guide you, and leave this place full of that prayer, "Lord, teach me to pray." I will exercise myself in it with you, however short the time may be: God does not consider length of time, but uprightness of heart. Humbled by the lukewarmness of our prayers, let us all, with one heart and one mind, form a holy resolution to learn by experience what are the promises made to prayer, that we may reap a blessed inheritance in that invisible world with which prayer alone, by the Word of God, puts us into communication; in that invisible world, nearer to some of us—further from others than they think or hope, and which, however that may be, in ten years, in twenty, in fifty, in a hundred—which would be immense—that is to say, in the twinkling of an eye—will open before all those of us who have built their hopes on Jesus Christ crucified and risen again from the dead. This is my earnest prayer for you, and if the Lord call me to Him, it is the inheritance I would wish to leave to each of you, beginning with my own dearly beloved family. Amen.

5

PREOCCUPATIONS WITH TRIVIAL MATTERS

My well beloved, who give me a proof of your fraternal affection in again coming to partake with me of the Lord's Supper, one of the things that would trouble the mind of a man who is contemplating death as at hand, if he were not encouraged in this, as in everything else, by the free grace of God in Jesus Christ, is the recollection of that part of his life that has been lost, if it has not been more than lost, in trifling matters, instead of being occupied by the great interests that alone ought to be constantly before the eyes of a Christian. For this reason I wish to call your attention for a few moments to the great evil of the Christian occupying himself too much with trifling interests. But here let me explain that we must not confound the undue preoccupation about trifling interests, with the necessary attention due to little things. We are required by God to busy ourselves about a multitude of little things, for it is especially of such that life is made up. The manner in which we fulfil our smaller duties is a measure of our piety, quite as true, and sometimes even more true, than the manner in which we fulfil the greater duties—because in little things we have only God, ourselves, and our family for witnesses; whereas in the accomplishment of the greater duties we are, as it were, upon a theatre where our pride may find but too much satisfaction in seeing itself flattered. Besides, nothing is either great or small in itself; it only becomes so by the spirit in which it is carried out. In the eyes of God, what we call little is often as great as what we call the greatest, and what we call great as little as what we call the least, since God is infinite and eternal. A faithful servant who, for the love of God, takes an affectionate care of the child confided to her by her master, performs an act which is very great in the sight of God, and will have its reward; and a statesman who, from self-love, aspires to the highest honours of wisdom and eloquence, does what seems very little in the sight of God, and may draw down upon him more shame in heaven than glory upon earth. What is really important is, to carry into all we do a great and elevated mind, always turned towards God, and disposed to do all in the view of eternity; so that, having God constantly present in our hearts, He may likewise always appear present in our words and actions—so that there may be nothing little, or terrestrial, or transitory in our whole life.

The example of God himself may serve to illustrate what I have just said. God makes no difference in the care He takes of great or little things. He forms a blade of grass or a flake of snow with as much care as He takes in ordering the proportions, the positions, and the movements of the planets; and whether He makes a grain of sand or plants a Mont Blanc,

He does it in a godlike manner—that is to say, perfectly. But this God, who sees nothing too small to deserve His attention, always has in view, even in His smallest works as well as in the greatest, eternity, His own kingdom, and glory; as He said himself, "I have created them for my glory." And there is absolutely nothing in all God's works, whether moral or physical, in which He has not manifested the immense weight of His infinite care and eternal interest. It was the same with Jesus— God made visible. Not only did He not neglect the poor little children that were brought to Him, and whom the apostles considered it beneath Him to bless, but He did not neglect even the fragments of bread and fish that remained, and would not allow anything to be lost, although He had just shewn that He could by a word, or even without a word, multiply the loaves and fishes at His will. And this is the same Jesus who accomplished the most prodigious works in His incarnation—in His redemption—in His passion—in His resurrection—and in His glorious ascension. But He does all in the same spirit; and whether He becomes incarnate, or ransoms us, or dies for us, or rises again, or ascends up to heaven—whether He stops to bless the little children, or to gather up the fragments of bread and fish, or to address the least word of consolation to the afflicted, or to offer a glass of cold water to one that is thirsty—He has always in view in each of His actions, God, eternity, and the glory of His Father; and it is in this light that Jesus Christ appears to us in all His works, as always having His head in heaven, although His feet were upon the earth, and saying of himself, "He who is in heaven." As all is great and noble in His soul, so also are all His works and thoughts.

Well, my dear friends, this is the example proposed for our imitation; it is thus that we should walk, always occupied, not with the little interests of the earth, still less with its lusts and sins, but with God, His glory, His love, and the work of Jesus Christ for the glory of God, and the salvation of men, as well as for our own. Made in the image and resemblance of God, we ought to be His followers; and in the least as well as in the greatest concerns of life, our predominant thought should always be God and eternity. Whatever the Christian may say or do, he should be always great before God, who weighs true grandeur. Painters represent the saints with a glory around them; there is nothing of the kind in Scripture, excepting for one saint in the Old Testament—this is the only exception. The saints carry their glory within them, and diffuse it wherever they pass. The Christian— wherever he is seen, in the street, in the drawing-room, at table, in prison, or at the height of greatness—should always inspire others with the opinion that he is a man seeking God, intent upon advancing the great interests of humanity, and who thinks it is not worth living for anything but to glorify God, and make all his successes and all his reverses contribute to that end; who is ready to leave this world as soon as his work in this respect is accomplished, and, like his Master, goes about doing good. Oh! how holy, how happy would such a Christian be, free from covetousness, from envy, from anxiety, and all that can disturb the soul I Walking always with God, how would he make the gospel honored! how victoriously would he put to silence gainsayers! and how many more souls would he bring to his Saviour by the humble influence of a holy life, than by the most powerful language!

But where are such Christians to be found? my God, where are they? How much easier it would be to find sincere men—true Christians, I mean—who, if they were called out of this world, would resign their souls into the Lord's hands—who really wait upon Him, but who allow themselves to be led away and unduly occupied by trifling interests—by the love of money—by the thirst for human glory—by their jealousy of a competitor—by the ardent desire for personal success—by an ambition that leads them beyond the path that God has marked out for them—by impatience under suffering—by their repugnance to submit to humiliations and crosses—by the great vexation that a word, perhaps even a word misunderstood, may cause them, or an insignificant accident, which at their death, perhaps even in an hour, will have left no trace! O my God, how few in number are consistent Christians! And this is the reason, my friends, that the gospel is so often compromised by those who profess it, and that it is so often said that, after all, the Christians pursue the same interests that others pursue, and that what disturbs others disturbs them too. And it is in this way, my friends, that the gospel is so often wounded by those who seek their peace and salvation in it, and who ought to employ all they have of life or strength to glorify God, going forward with their head elevated—their head in heaven like Jesus, while their feet are upon the earth—but breathing in heaven and finding there the spring of all their actions and the strength of all their life.

If you knew, my friends, how all these illusions disappear when death approaches—how very little all that is little appears—how that alone which is great before God appears great, how much we regret not having lived for God as Jesus lived, and how much we wish, if we had to begin life again, to live a more serious life, more full of Jesus Christ, of His Word, of His example,—if you knew it, you would at this moment put your hand to the work, you would supplicate God to make your conduct consistent with your sentiments

and your faith; you would succeed in your efforts, as so many
have succeeded, because they cried to God, and formed sincere
resolutions before Him: and this handful of God's children
now assembled in this room, around this bed of suffering,
and probably of death, these Christians, with all their miseries
and all their languor, would do more for the advancement of
God's kingdom, and for the good of humanity, than a compact
crowd possessing all possible gifts; and they would do things
so much the greater, that all thoughts of vainglory would be
for ever banished from their heart. This is my ardent prayer
for you, and it is the prayer that I entreat you to offer to God
for me, that during the time that still remains for me, whether
it be long or short, I may think only of living for the glory
of God and for the good of my fellow men, which will at the
same time be living for my own eternal happiness. Amen

About The Author

Adolphe-Louis-Frédéric-Théodore Monod was born in Copenhagen on January 21st, 1802, where his father was pastor of the French church. His elder brother was Frédéric Monod. Educated at Paris and Geneva, he began his life-work in 1825 as founder and pastor of a Protestant church in Naples, moving to Lyon in 1827. Here his evangelical preaching, and especially a sermon on the duties of communicants (Qui doit communier?), led to his deposition by the Catholic Minister of education and religion. Instead of leaving Lyon he began to preach in a hall and then in a chapel.

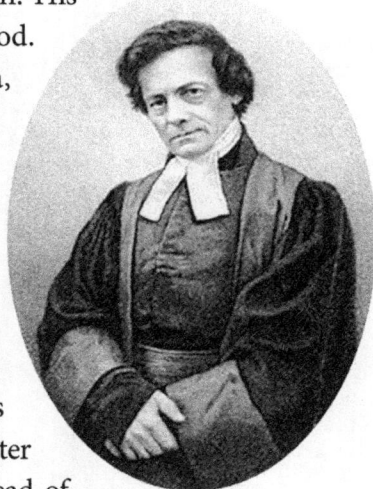

On September 2nd, 1829 he married Hannah Honyman in Lyon. They had seven children.

In 1836 he took a professorship in the theological college of Montauban, removing in 1847 to Paris as preacher at the Oratoire. He died there on April 6th, 1856.

Monod was undoubtedly the foremost Protestant churchman and preacher of 19th century France. He published three volumes of sermons in 1830, another, *La Crédulité de l'incrédule* in 1844, and two more in 1855. Two further volumes appeared after his death. One of his most influential books was the posthumous, *Les Adieux d'Adolphe Monod à ses Amis et à l'Église* (*Adolphe Monod's Farewell to his Friends and to his Church* from which this book's content is extracted).

THE MISSION OF GREAT CHRISTIAN BOOKS

The ministry of Great Christian Books was established to glorify The Lord Jesus Christ and to be used by Him to expand and edify the kingdom of God while we occupy and anticipate Christ's glorious return. Great Christian Books will seek to accomplish this mission by publishing Gospel literature which is biblically faithful, relevant, and practically applicable to many of the serious spiritual needs of mankind upon the beginning of this new millennium. To do so we will always seek to boldly incorporate the truths of Scripture, especially those which were largely articulated as a body of theology during the Protestant Reformation of the sixteenth century and ensuing years. We gladly join our voice in the proclamations of— Scripture Alone, Faith Alone, Grace Alone, Christ Alone, and God's Glory Alone!

Our ministry seeks the blessing of our God as we seek His face to both confirm and support our labors for Him. Our prayers for this work can be summarized by two verses from the Book of Psalms:

"...let the beauty of the LORD our God be upon us, And establish the work of our hands for us; Yes, establish the work of our hands." —Psalm 90:17

"Not unto us, O LORD, not unto us, but to your name give glory." —Psalm 115:1

Great Christian Books appreciates the financial support of anyone who shares our burden and vision for publishing literature which combines sound Bible doctrine and practical exhortation in an age when too few so-called "Christian" publications do the same. We thank you in advance for any assistance you can give us in our labors to fulfill this important mission. May God bless you.

For a catalog of other great
Christian books including
additional titles by
Adolphe Monod
contact us in
any of the following ways:

write us at:
Great Christian Books
160 37th Street
Lindenhurst, NY 11757

call us at:
631. 956. 0998

find us online:
www.greatchristianbooks.com

email us at:
mail@greatchristianbooks.com